Garstang
Past

at heart  publications

The Garstang
Courier

First published in 2007 by
At Heart Ltd, 32 Stamford Street, Altrincham,
Cheshire, WA14 1EY
in conjunction with
Garstang Courier, 7 Pringle Court, Park Hill
Road, Garstang, PR31LN.

Printed and bound by Bell & Bain Ltd., Glasgow

ISBN: 978-1-84547-137-8

Introduction

October 4, 2007, saw the publication of my eight hundredth "Reverent Reflections" article for the *Garstang Courier.* That is a lot of words, a lot of newsprint and a lot of pictures loaned to us by the people of Garstang and District.

The use of three or four pictures for each article comes to over two and a half thousand items you have shared with me over the last fifteen years. This publication is, therefore, a tribute and thanks to you, the readers.

Through this area of England now known as Garstang and District there have, throughout the ages, flowed the tides that make up the history of England. The Romans moved over it between their settlements at Ribchester, Walton-le-Dale and Lancaster; the Vikings swept across the Irish Sea to carry the Saxon settlers there; the Scots under Bruce came down in the fourteenth century, burning and slaying as far south as Chorley; the armies of both sides passed and repassed during the Civil War; the Scots came down again, to meet defeat at Preston in 1715, and again in 1745 when they turned back from Derby signalling the final dissipation of Jacobite hopes.

Throughout the ages, the names of the men and women of this area are to be found on the muster rolls of those who rushed to defend their country at times of national crisis – to fight against the Scots at Flodden in 1513; to drive off the Spaniards in 1588; and to guard our shores against Napolean and Hitler. It is to them and their successors that we owe all that is shown on the pages of this book.

It is rightly said that one picture can convey more than a thousand words, hence why this book is composed of many pictures and few words.

Canon Ron Greenall, October 2007

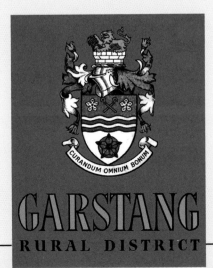

● Garstang Rural District Council Crest is a reminder of former local government days

About Garstang

The town of Garstang, which occupies a pleasant position on the banks of the River Wyre, is steeped in antiquity. The name was anciently spelt 'Gayr-stang', said to derive from the Domesday Survey where it is called Cherestanc.

For many years Garstang was a most important market town, also noted for its cattle and horse fairs, which were held annually in November. The Market House, built in 1843, is still in use, and the market is held each Thursday in this building and the main street adjoining, under the auspices of the Garstang Town Trust, a body appointed to take over the functions previously exercised by the Corporation, which was dissolved in 1886.

The road from the south enters Garstang over the Wyre Bridge, which is a substantial stone structure erected about 200 years ago to replace a narrow old bridge built by the Earl of Derby, probably about the time Greenhalgh Castle was erected. This ancient bridge existed long before the railway, the trunk road or the M6 motorway. It was the entry point to Garstang for people on foot, on horseback or travelling by stagecoach.

Looking east from this bridge, there is a very fine view along the River Wyre and in the distance one can see the hilly and finely wooded parish of Barnacre, and the higher points of the Bleasdale and Wyresdale Fells. Looking west, a good view is obtained of the stone aqueduct which carries the Preston-Lancaster-Kendal Canal over the river. It is a fine piece of engineering work and well worth a visit.

Proceeding up Bridge Street from Wyre Bridge, the road opens out into the Market Place and High Street, which is the principal shopping centre. On the east side of High Street stands the old Town Hall, which was the administrative centre of the former Corporation of Garstang. The original building was demolished in 1755, but when its replacement was damaged in a fire in 1939, the new building was restored in keeping with its original characteristics. The current building, which is now vested in the Garstang Town Trust, is used for commercial purposes and the upper storey is leased to the British Legion as Club Headquarters. The regalia of the old Corporation, consisting of halberds, staff and historic records, are housed in this building.

The Market Cross, restored in 1897, stands in the centre of the Market Place and is a relic of ancient days, so much so that there appears to be no trace of the date it was erected.

● Bowgreave Rise, the entrance to Garstang before the new A6

● Another Bowgreave shot

• It's a long hill into town...

• Then it goes downhill...

● Then you reach the Church Inn and St. Mary & Michael's Church

The Roman Catholic Church, dedicated to Saint Mary and Saint Michael, is a handsome Gothic structure, from a design by the elder Pugin, and actually stands in Bonds, just over the parish boundary. It superseded the chapel erected in 1784, which was later converted into the Garstang Institute.

The church was opened in 1858. It is built of stone and consists of a nave and aisle, supported by a row of fine pillars with pointed arches. The altar is Caen stone and the windows are of beautiful stained glass. There is a fine tower and spire. Adjoining the church are the Presbytery and burial ground.

Postcards sent in by readers of my regular column in the Garstang Courier make up many of the pictures in this book.

The period between 1900 and 1914 is described as the golden age of postcards.

In the pre-telephone era and before newspaper pictures became commonplace, postcards were the cheapest and most reliable method of sending messages and illustrating local and national news and events.

It is no exaggeration to say that every conceivable subject seems to be depicted or satirised upon.

Did you know that while picture postcards were in common use in Europe, in general from the 1870's, the post office in Britain did not officially approve them until 1894?

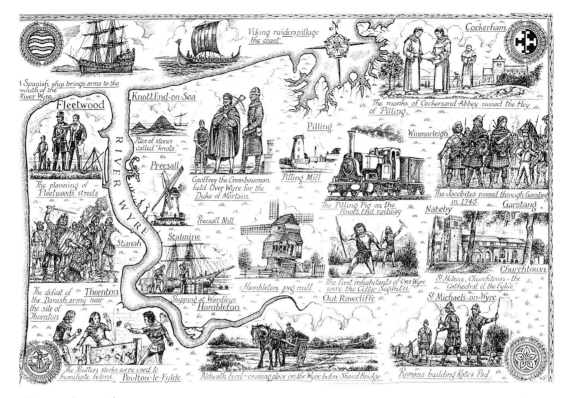

• Illustrated map of our area

• Greetings from Garstang postcard

• The Market Cross, which
was restored in 1897

• An ariel view of the Cross in Garstang

● Children at the Market Cross on Coronation Day, June 22, 1911

• The local bobbies compare notes

• The District Bank in Market Place, opposite the Royal Oak

• The Cattle Fair, circa 1898

● The Market and Cross dominates the town centre

● As do the shops on High Street, Market Street, Bridge Street and Church Street

In 1750 the Town Hall was destroyed by fire and most of the old historical records were also destroyed. The new building to rise from the ashes was a much more sturdy construction, which served the town well for hundreds of years until it was once again involved in a fire in 1939.

The stonework was preserved in the rebuilding, and the position of a police cell that was situated under the building can still be seen today.

Historically, the danger of fire was always very real for the 160 houses in Garstang, as in 1820 three quarters of them had thatched roofs.

● The Town Hall after a disastrous fire in 1939

• Market Place in carriage days

• Market Day in Garstang in 1904

• And again in 1905

• Bowler hats, caps and straw boaters all on parade
in this Market Day scene from 1908

• A market day scene from the 1920s

• Just look at these market day fashions!

● A view of the market from the junction
of Church Street and Market Place in 1910

Shops have as vital a part to play in the pictures shown here as they do in everyday life. It was from the local shops and the market that we got our orange and soap boxes.

For a variety of reasons it was in the traditional corner shop where most people shopped. The multiple grocers closed at 6pm except Wednesday when they closed for half day.

The corner shop didn't close until the owner went to bed at say 10pm every day including Sundays and even then, if urgent, she (inevitably it was a housewife whose husband had another job) would serve regular customers at the back door.

The type of urgency would be a bottle of medicine sold usually in two penny bottles from cards of twelve hanging all around the shop. Camphorated oil, eucalyptus oil, olive oil, oil of peppermint, cubes of camphor, headache powders, teething powders for children, liver salts, rheumatism pills, sciatica pills, Beecham's pills, bandages, lint and sticky plasters were all available and many others.

All housewives were skilled at home doctoring and made their diagnoses with the corroboration of friendly neighbours and were usually correct.

There was of course the shop counter on which stood a pair of brass scales with a set of brass weights graduating from half of an ounce to one pound, and a further set of more robust cast steel scales stood on an upturned soap box beside the counter with weights of a quarter pound to 14 pounds.

• Storey's shop, Market Place

• Storey's delivery cart

• A thriving market stall before the war

• F. Gardner's, the boot and shoemakers

• All's quiet on High Street

● Hartley's Ironmongers, High Street

● Butler's the Saddlers, High Street

● Bartlett's family grocers circa 1905, now the location of Barclays Bank

- The Eagle & Child

- American visitors to the Eagle & Child

• Looking down the High Street from
the Eagle & Child in 1908

● The roof timbers of a house on High Street

● Stoops Hall at the
turn of the century

• Bridge Street

● Bridge Street garage, thatched shops and the Golden Ball Inn

● An early procession on Bridge Street

• Children playing on Bridge Street

• The Royal Oak and shops on Church Street

● Church Street looking east

• Old cottages on Church Street in 1922, on the site
that is now occupied by St. Thomas' Church carpark

• Locals take a look at the huge
snowdrift on Church Street in 1940

● More snow on Church Street in 1940

In 1437 a licence was granted to the inhabitants of Garstang to hold divine service in the chapel of Holy Trinity, which was located on a site adjoining the present Market House. In 1769 the church was rebuilt on the present site in Church Street and was consecrated in the name of St. Thomas. It was created a separate parish in 1881.

The present church is built of stone, and formerly consisted of a nave, chancel, galleries and a square tower, but the galleries were taken out in 1946. There is a fine stained glass window above the altar and the organ is one of the best in the district. A burial ground was presented to the church in 1845 by F. W. Keppel Esq., whose successor provided land for an extension at a later date. The vicarage adjoins the church.

• St. Thomas' in the snow, 1987

• This pre-war image shows children waiting
at the gates of St. Thomas' Church

• Two schoolboys on Church Street

• The Kings
Arms Hotel

• Early tourists at the Cat House Inn

• Staff at
Garstang's
Co-op store

• The Punch Bowl, Churchtown, circa 1902

● The Market Cross at Churchtown

• The Hotel Excel

● An AA patrolman pictured on the A6 outside the hotel around 1928

• An early bus from Garstang to Preston

• A very early bus on Bowgreave Hill

● An early motorcar at Barnacre Lodge

●The A6 at Broughton Crossroads in the 1920s

● Going nowhere. A bus is caught in
a snowdrift on the A6, January 1940

● The M6 takes shape locally

● More work at Scorton

In the early days of motoring all traffic came through the centre of town, but in 1926 a bypass road took traffic away from the town and did relieve congestion as this became the main A6.

In 1959 the Preston Bypass, Britain's first motorway, was built and this was soon followed by the development of the M6 North. Three miles north of Garstang you see the wonderful sweep of the Snow Hill Bridge and St Peter's Church spire, pictured here during the M6 construction.

● Construction of the motorway bridge by St. Peter's, Scorton

● Some of the first traffic on the M6

The railway line from Preston Junction to Lancaster opened on June 25, 1840, however due to local opposition, the station serving Garstang had to be positioned two miles away from the town.

A spur was later taken to Garstang Town Station but the opposition to the original main line route into the town itself cost loss in trade and development.

● Garstang & Catterall Station

• A snowplough attempts to clear the Nateby Line, 1940

● Steaming into Garstang & Catterall Station

● Barton & Broughton Station

• A steam train approaches Wadacre Crossing

• Brock Station

Mention Garstang to anyone and you will most likely be questioned about the Pilling Pig.

Way back in 1864, track was laid between Garstang Town Station and Pilling. The service began operation on December 5, 1870.

In 1908 the service was extended to Knott End on Sea and became known as the Garstang to Knott End Railway.

One of its engines, the Farmer's Friend, had a very shrill whistle and became known as the Pilling Pig. Later the nickname was given to the whole operation of the G & KR railway.

By 1930 all passenger services on this line ceased with only freight services remaining, which locals continued to refer to as the Pilling Pig.

● The line from Garstang Town Station to Pilling

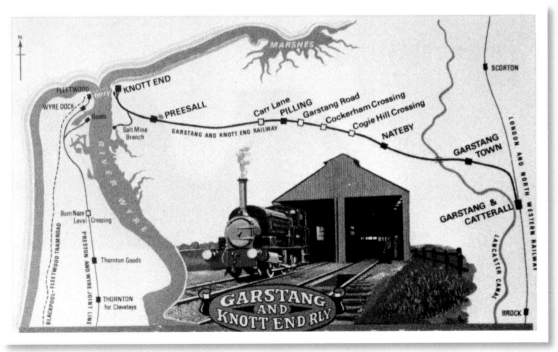

● The route of the Pilling Pig Railway

• A pastoral scene from Bowgreave taken around 1912

● Houses on West View

• Pump Street, Claughton, around 1924

• Bonds Lane looking south

At the start of the 20th century the manorial rights and ownership of much property in Garstang were in the hands of the Keppel family. To ease his job, the agent who had the task of collecting house rents numbered the properties according to his records.

This number was attached to the inside of the front door, while the house number designated by Garstang Town Council went on the front of the front door. Confused?

The then residents were not, for in those days everybody knew everybody and it was enough to just put the name and Garstang on the letter or package.

In October 1919, Major Keppel sold off much of his property in Garstang. Until then firm control of building and development had been maintained by the Keppel family, and Garstang was known far and wide as 'The Finished Town'. What a difference today with all the new building in and around Garstang.

• Boys playing on Croston Road. The United Reformed Church in Croston Road was erected in 1778 and a Sunday School and caretaker's cottage were added in 1903.

• Manor thatched cottages in Garstang

● Catterall Post Office

● Scorton Square

●The centre of Scorton

● St. John's Church, Calder Vale

● Calder Vale

● Another picturesque view of Calder Vale

•The remains of Greenhalgh Castle are still standing

• Greenhalgh Castle's remains in the distance

Just to the east of Garstang, on top of a small knoll, are the scanty remains of one of the few castles in the county – Greenhalgh Castle, built in 1490 by the first Thomas Stanley, Earl of Derby, to protect the lands, formerly belonging to the supporters of Richard III, which had been granted to the Earl by Henry VII.

During the Civil War the castle was held for the King, and earned a place in history as being the penultimate stronghold to hold out against the forces of Parliament. In fact it was only the death of its governor that caused the defenders to surrender.

The Mill & Weir, Garstang.

• The old cornmill, Garstang

● Fluke Hall, Pilling

● Moss Lane gasworks

● Brock House and Mill

• Workers from Collinson's Agricultural Engineers and General Smiths

● Haymaking at Nateby

● Haymaking in Barnacre

● Garstang canal basin

RIVER WYRE, GARSTANG.

● The Wyre Bridge, pastoral Wyre and cornmill

● Wyre Bridge and the Weir

● The frozen Wyre at St. Michael's

If you are among the rare few privileged to enter St. Michael's Church belfry and examine the members of the carillon you will find three bells. One dates back to 1663, one to 1742, and one as far back as 1458.

We know this because this particular bell has the following inscription:

"In the year 1458 this bell was made and given by Catherine de Bernieules, Lady of Neufchatel".

It is thought that the bell was intended for a church in Picardy, France, and for some reason found its way to Lancashire, perhaps in the 16th century.

River Wyre, Garstang,

● Two boys fishing as on the River Wyre in 1921

• Rowers pass under Wyre Bridge

From monastic times, one tenth of the produce or livestock was given to the Abbey, and from this the scholastic and charitable work of the church was funded. This produce was known as a 'tithe', and in Garstang, the tithe would have been given to Cockersand's Abbey.

With the dissolution of the monasteries, much of the tithe was transferred to the local church, in many cases providing for the stipend of the vicar or rector.

This produce was then stored in ancient tithe barns, such as the one that stood by the canal basin in Garstang. The barn was in a dilapidated state by the middle of the century, but was thankfully restored at the end of the 1970s and redeveloped as a museum, bar and restaurant.

• Down by the riverside long ago

• Children outside Tithebarn

Whit Monday would always see the return of many Garstonians who had since moved to other parts. Families held great parties and celebrations on this day and people flocked into town from much of the surrounding area. A real festival atmosphere was enjoyed and included fairground rides, sports and sideshows on the Royal Oak Field (now part of the extension of St. Thomas' Churchyard).

Until the First World War there were two separate processions on this day, the Anglican and Nonconformist walk, and the Roman Catholic walk. After the war, the processions united and eventually the Whit Festival became a children's festival rather than a religious walk.

With the introduction of the late May bank holiday weekend, the children's festival was standardised on this day, with Churchtown and Catterall holding their own festivals on the Saturdays either side of this, allowing extended use of the floats and banners.

• Children pass the Wyre Café, a part of the Whitsuntide Festival in 1950

• Whit Monday 1950

● Leading a merry dance

● Hold on to your hats

● Whit Monday at the turn of the century

● A Whit Monday gathering, 1900

- The Festival Queen on the Royal Oak field

- Garstang Festival children, 1937

• Another great Whit procession postcard

• A float preparation outside the Wheatsheaf

• A festival group outside the Eagle & Child

• The fairground on the Farmer's Arms car park

• It's the Whit Monday Queen in 1950

• Winter Wonderland

• Another happy group of children from the 1950 celebrations

• Here comes the daisy chain

• Yet more dancers and musicians, 1950

• In praise of old English lavender

• A last taste of the 1950 Whit Festival lemons

• Another Whit Monday picture from 1950

May Queens, May Day celebrations involving the decoration of horses, and maypole dancing were always an integral part of early summer celebrations in and around Garstang.

Between 1918 and the start of the Second World War, passengers on the West Coast line between London and Scotland would look out for the maypole close to Scorton Station as they passed by on the train.

● A bevy of Whit queens over the years - their saches marking their individual year of reign

● Maypole dancing in Scorton in the fifties

Bilsborrow Coronation Festival,
6th. June 1953.

• The brass band plays at Bilsborrow Coronation
Festival, 1953

• Calder Vale band at Barnacre Lodge around 1923

● Calder Vale band in full uniform in the mid-1930s

● Churchtown Festival, 1937

• Coronation Day fair at Churchtown in 1911

• Another picture of the Coronation Festival, June 22, 1911

The Old Woman Who Lived in a Shoe

• A Churchtown Festival float

• A Humpty Dumpty float from Churchtown Festival

• Morris Dancers from Churchtown School during the 1960s

● Stalmine School Morris Dancers

● Group 1 Class from St. Thomas' School around 1902

● St. Thomas School class of 1911

● St. Thomas' class photograph during the 1920s, with headmaster, Tommy Austin

The building that once housed the old Grammar School lies at the north end of the town and is today occupied by the Arts Centre.

It was built in 1756 when the Lord of the Manor, Sir Edward Walpole, donated the land for the school's construction. The annual salary of the first headmaster was just three pounds and seven shillings.

The school produced some outstanding academic and sporting results, but by the mid-1800s the building had fallen into a dilapidated state. However it wasn't until 1928, when long-serving headmaster, Joseph Irwin, finally retired, that the Grammar School was closed for good.

Irwin had taken up the headship in 1898. He was a strict disciplinarian but a good teacher, and a very well respected Garstonian.

In 1929 the building was reopened as a domestic science and woodwork centre for the other schools in the area. Today it is the property of the Garstang Town Trust and is used extensively by the community for arts and social activities.

• Garstang Grammar School boys from around 1910

• The Grammar School's football team, circa 1923

St. Mary & Michael's School football team, 1922

● Pilling C. of E. football team, 1933. Pictured from left to right: (Back row) Robert Taylor, John Taylor, F. J. Sobee (schoolmaster), Charlie Carter, Dick Preston (trainer), Dennis Martin, Richard Jenkinson. (Middle row) John Shepherd, Edward Anyon, William Jenkinson, Fred Ronson. (Front row) William Aldren, Kenneth Billington, Fred Thornton.

• Nateby School over 40 years ago

• A girls-only sewing and domestic science lesson, Nateby

• Garstang tennis club in bygone days

Conclusion

I conclude with an article on "The Household Round" which I first used in the *Garstang Courier* in 1991 and which I think sums up nicely how things used to be done.

Monday was the washing day. The dolly tub, posser and wringers came into their own today, as did the starch and dolly blue. The rack and maiden were full of clothes drying on a wet day and on the outside line in the yard if the weather was fine.

Tuesday was ironing day. Box irons were a vital part of this. The inner irons were put on the fire to heat and then transferred into the iron itself.

Wednesday was a baking day. Normally we had a potato pie when we came home from school at dinnertime and then at teatime all the baking for the week would be on the table and we could help ourselves to anything going.

Thursday the bedrooms were cleaned, mattresses turned and pummelled and downstairs cleaning commenced to be completed on Friday.

On this day steps and back yard were also swilled and cleaned, as were the windowsills and downstairs windows. The steps were donkey stoned and the windowsills given a polish of cardinal red.

Saturday was shopping day, and if you left going to the market until very late in the afternoon then you really did get a good deal fruit and veg.

Sunday was for church, family visiting, and of course the special Sunday dinner. On Monday the pattern started again just as last week.